Success
is getting up
just one more time
than you fall
down.

To _____

From _____

Also by
Barbara Milo Ohrbach

The Scented Room

*The Scented Room
Gardening Notebook*

Antiques at Home

A Token of Friendship

Memories of Childhood

A Bouquet of Flowers

A Cheerful Heart

The Spirit of America

Merry Christmas

Simply Flowers

Happy Birthday

All Things Are Possible

∾ Pass the Word ∾

By BARBARA MILO OHRBACH

CLARKSON POTTER/PUBLISHERS NEW YORK

Copyright © 1995 by Barbara Milo Ohrbach

Every effort has been made to locate the copyright holders of
materials used in this book. Should there be any omissions or
errors, we apologize and shall be pleased to make the appropriate
acknowledgements in future editions.

All rights reserved. No part of this book may be
reproduced or transmitted in any form or by any means,
electronic or mechanical, including photocopying,
recording, or by any information storage and retrieval system,
without permission in writing from the publisher.

Published by Clarkson N. Potter/Inc., 201 East 50th Street,
New York, New York 10022.
Member of the Crown Publishing Group.

Random House, Inc. New York, Toronto, London,
Sydney, Auckland

CLARKSON N. POTTER, POTTER, and colophon are
trademarks of Clarkson N. Potter, Inc.

Manufactured in the United States of America

Design by Justine Strasberg

Library of Congress Cataloging-in-Publication Data
All things are possible–pass the word / [compiled] by
Barbara Milo Ohrbach
1. Quotations, English. 2. Quotations. I. Ohrbach, Barbara Milo.
    PN6081.A53 1995   94-37344
    082--dc20   CIP

ISBN 0-517-88426-7
10 9 8 7 6

I am so fortunate to have been surrounded by encouraging, energetic, and enthusiastic people all my life. I would like to thank my husband, all my friends, and my associates at Clarkson Potter, who helped make this book possible. Charles Acree, Beth and John Allen, Gayle Benderoff, Sam Chapnick, Cathy Collins, Susan DeStaebler, Phyllis Fleiss, Deborah Geltman, Tim Girvin, Janice Hamilton, Allison Hanes, Annetta Hanna, Lisa Keim, Howard Klein, Steve Magnuson, Patti McCarthy, Jean Dimore Markovitz, Barbara Marks, Teresa Nicholas, Mel Ohrbach, Ed Otto, Andrea C. Peabbles, Pam Romano, Pat Sadowsky, Wendy Schuman, Lauren Shakely, Gail Shanks, Michelle Sidrane, Harry Singer, Tina Strasberg, Robin Strashun, Jane Treuhaft, Shirley Wohl, Helen Zimmerman.

And to my nieces and nephews — Nanny would be so proud to see you all growing up, embracing the love of life and its challenges in the spirit that she passed on to all of us.

Introduction

"THERE IS NO SUCH WORD AS CAN'T."

My mother said those words at least once a day when I was growing up. They wove through my childhood and adolescence like a melody. "I can't," I would say. "You can," she would answer. You see, my mother always looked on the bright side—a trait viewed with some skepticism in our family. I know now that it couldn't have been easy for her, a harried 1950s housewife, but she never gave up.

I whined and argued—she persevered. And when

6

pushed, she'd fall back on a favorite quote by the Duc de la Rochefoucauld: "Nothing is impossible; there are ways that lead to everything."

She set a wonderful example. Eventually, she taught me to believe in myself and that if I set out to accomplish something, I would succeed! And, if I didn't, well, tomorrow was a fresh, new day and I could try again.

And in the end, she left me something very precious— a firm conviction that the world is full of wonderful possibilities. That there are few things in life that can't be tackled successfully. And that, indeed, there is no such word as *can't*. I had become an optimist!

But today, I find it's almost too easy to be pessimistic. We live in a complex, uncertain world that seems out of our control and can sometimes make us feel powerless. It's hard enough to face the everyday obstacles, let alone think about trying to make a difference in the big picture. But we must not give into this feeling. One person doing something *can* make a difference.

7

In the nineteenth century, Goethe wrote, "Let everyone sweep in front of his door and the whole world will be clean." And recently, Mother Teresa said, "If you can't feed a hundred people, then feed just one." We must have faith in ourselves and what we can accomplish. Then we can pass on this feeling of empowerment, enriching our lives and the lives of others as well.

Over the years, whenever I wasn't feeling up to par, I'd read a little something to pick up my spirits. Eventually I accumulated a collection of wonderfully uplifting thoughts that made me feel good! Now, they're all here, together in this book. The quotes range from ancient times to the present day, but their positive, hopeful message is ageless. I hope they encourage and challenge you to do something you've always wanted to do but never attempted. Remember that all things are possible— and optimism is meant to be shared. If you pass the word, you will help someone else to believe it, too.

—Barbara Milo Ohrbach

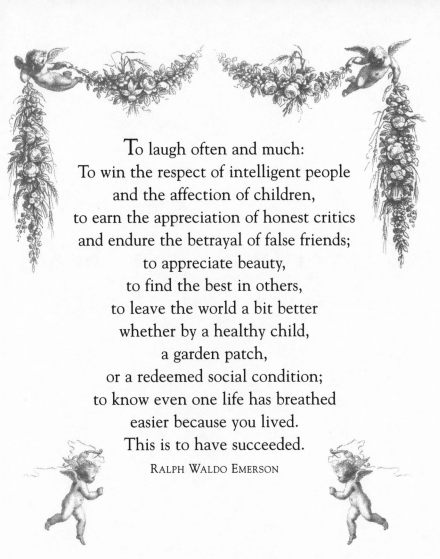

To laugh often and much:
To win the respect of intelligent people
and the affection of children,
to earn the appreciation of honest critics
and endure the betrayal of false friends;
to appreciate beauty,
to find the best in others,
to leave the world a bit better
whether by a healthy child,
a garden patch,
or a redeemed social condition;
to know even one life has breathed
easier because you lived.
This is to have succeeded.

RALPH WALDO EMERSON

*N*ever bend your head.
Always hold it high.

Look the world straight in the eye. HELEN KELLER

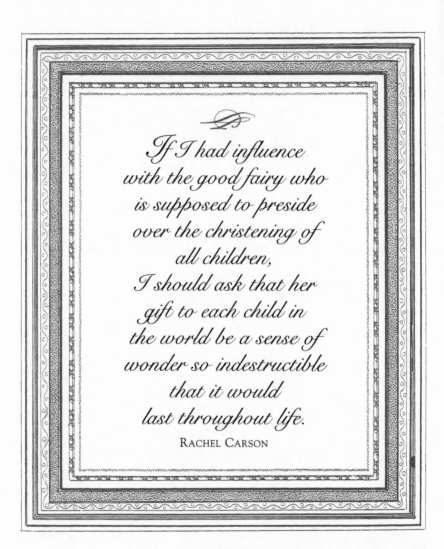

*If I had influence
with the good fairy who
is supposed to preside
over the christening of
all children,
I should ask that her
gift to each child in
the world be a sense of
wonder so indestructible
that it would
last throughout life.*

RACHEL CARSON

The best way to make your dreams come true
is to wake up.

PAUL VALÉRY

Keep your eyes on the stars,
keep your feet on the ground.

THEODORE ROOSEVELT

Beware what you set your heart upon.
For it surely shall be yours.

RALPH WALDO EMERSON

Far away there in the sunshine are my highest
aspirations. I may not reach them, but I can look up
and see their beauty, believe in them and try to follow
where they lead.

LOUISA MAY ALCOTT

There is no end. There is no beginning.
There is only the infinite passion of life.

FEDERICO FELLINI

Our obligation is to give meaning to life and in doing
so to overcome the passive, indifferent life.

ELIE WIESEL

So many worlds, so much to do.
So little done, such things to be.

ALFRED, LORD TENNYSON

Know the true value of time; snatch, seize, and enjoy
every moment of it.

LORD CHESTERFIELD

I never remember feeling tired by work, though
idleness exhausts me completely.

ARTHUR CONAN DOYLE

$\mathscr{I}$ still find each
day too short for all the
thoughts I want to think,
all the walks I want to take,
all the books I want to read,
and all the friends I want
to see. The longer I live,
the more my mind dwells
upon the beauty and the
wonder of the world.

JOHN BURROUGHS

$\mathcal{A}$ll things are possible

to him that believes.

MARK 9:23

A happy person is not a person in a certain set of circumstances, but rather a person with a certain set of attitudes.

HUGH DOWNS

The way I see it, if you want the rainbow, you gotta put up with the rain.

DOLLY PARTON

There are only two ways to live your life. One is as though nothing is a miracle. The other is as though everything is a miracle.

ALBERT EINSTEIN

Act as if you were already happy and that will tend to make you happy.

DALE CARNEGIE

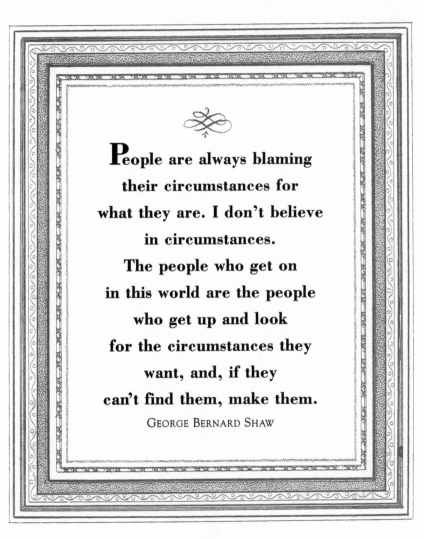

People are always blaming
their circumstances for
what they are. I don't believe
in circumstances.
The people who get on
in this world are the people
who get up and look
for the circumstances they
want, and, if they
can't find them, make them.

GEORGE BERNARD SHAW

Life begets life. Energy creates energy.
It is by spending oneself that one becomes rich.

SARAH BERNHARDT

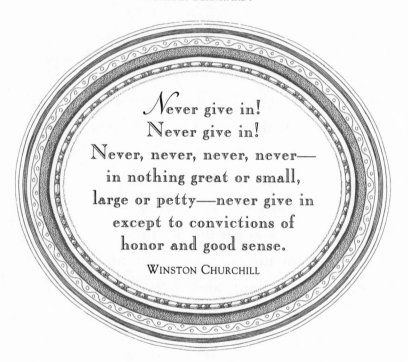

*N*ever give in!
Never give in!
Never, never, never, never—
in nothing great or small,
large or petty—never give in
except to convictions of
honor and good sense.

WINSTON CHURCHILL

Courage is contagious. When a brave man takes a
stand, the spines of others are often stiffened.

BILLY GRAHAM

Don't give in! Make your own trail.

KATHARINE HEPBURN

Nothing great was ever achieved without enthusiasm.

RALPH WALDO EMERSON

You may have to fight a battle more than once to win it.

MARGARET THATCHER

The time is always right to do what is right.

MARTIN LUTHER KING JR.

You can't win any game unless you are ready to win.

CONNIE MACK

Nothing in life is to be feared. It is only to be understood.

MARIE CURIE

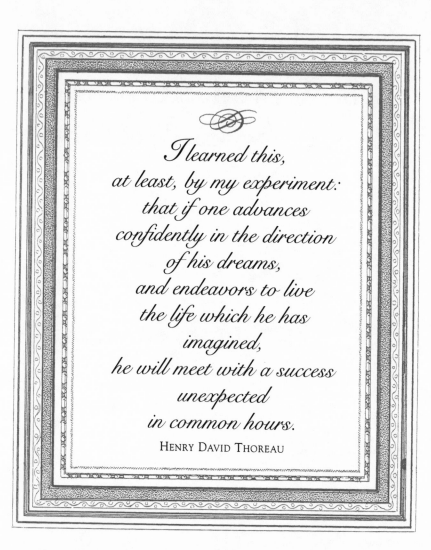

*I learned this,
at least, by my experiment:
that if one advances
confidently in the direction
of his dreams,
and endeavors to live
the life which he has
imagined,
he will meet with a success
unexpected
in common hours.*

HENRY DAVID THOREAU

It is a very funny thing about life: if you refuse to accept anything but the best you very often get it.

W. SOMERSET MAUGHAM

 That's one small step for man, one giant leap for mankind.

NEIL A. ARMSTRONG

Change is always powerful.
Let your hook be always cast.
In the pool where you least expect it, will be a fish.

OVID

If you think you can, you can.
And if you think you can't, you're right.

MARY KAY ASH

I think that if you shake the tree, you ought to be around when the fruit falls to pick it up.

MARY CASSATT

We must welcome the future, remembering that soon it will be the past; and we must respect the past, knowing that once it was all that was humanly possible.

GEORGE SANTAYANA

Nothing is so contagious as enthusiasm.

EDWARD GEORGE BULWER-LYTTON

Hope springs eternal in the human breast.

ALEXANDER POPE

When one door is shut, another opens.

MIGUEL DE CERVANTES

One of the things I learned the hard way was it does not pay to get discouraged. Keeping busy and making optimism a way of life can restore your faith in yourself.

LUCILLE BALL

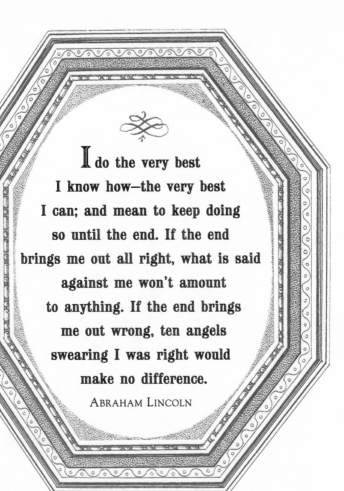

I do the very best
I know how—the very best
I can; and mean to keep doing
so until the end. If the end
brings me out all right, what is said
against me won't amount
to anything. If the end brings
me out wrong, ten angels
swearing I was right would
make no difference.

ABRAHAM LINCOLN

$\mathcal{W}$hatever you can do, or

$\mathcal{L}$ive each day as if your

dream you can, Begin it.

life had just begun.

JOHANN WOLFGANG VON GOETHE

Even if you're on the right track you'll get run over if you just sit there.

WILL ROGERS

Keep on going and the chances are that you will stumble on something, perhaps when you are least expecting it. I have never heard of anyone stumbling on something sitting down.

CHARLES F. KETTERING

Life is like a ten-speed bike. Most of us have gears we never use.

CHARLES SCHULTZ

You can't break a bad habit by throwing it out the window. You've got to walk it slowly down the stairs.

MARK TWAIN

Since you have to do the things you have to do, be wise enough to do some of the things you want to do.

MALCOLM FORBES

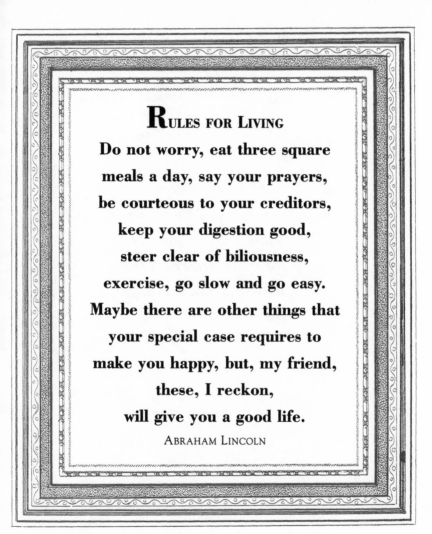

Rules for Living

Do not worry, eat three square
meals a day, say your prayers,
be courteous to your creditors,
keep your digestion good,
steer clear of biliousness,
exercise, go slow and go easy.
Maybe there are other things that
your special case requires to
make you happy, but, my friend,
these, I reckon,
will give you a good life.

ABRAHAM LINCOLN

Pessimism is a waste of time.

NORMAN COUSINS

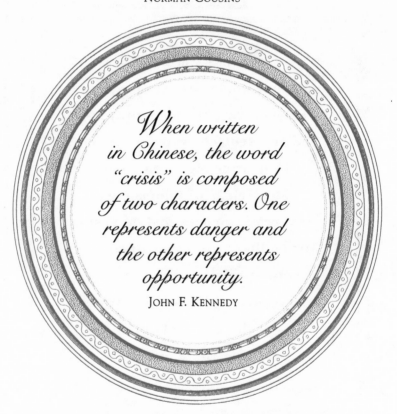

When written in Chinese, the word "crisis" is composed of two characters. One represents danger and the other represents opportunity.

JOHN F. KENNEDY

Pessimism leads to weakness, optimism to power.

WILLIAM JAMES

Ninety percent of inspiration is perspiration.

ANONYMOUS

Anybody can do anything that he imagines.

HENRY FORD

Always take hold of things by the smooth handle.

THOMAS JEFFERSON

At the side of the everlasting why, is a yes,
and a yes, and a yes.

E. M. FORSTER

If it exists, it's possible.

JOHN P. GRIER

The game isn't over till it's over.

YOGI BERRA

The word impossible is not in my dictionary.

NAPOLEON BONAPARTE

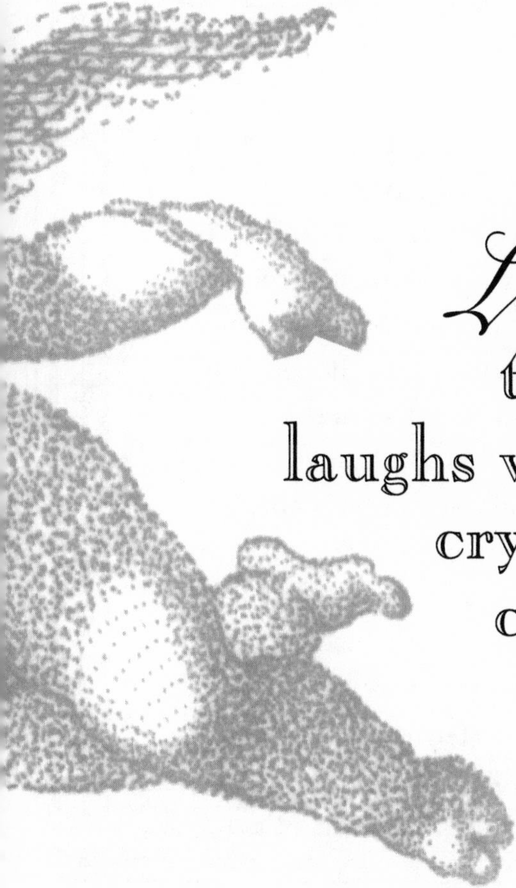

Laugh and
the world
laughs with you,
cry and you
cry alone.

ELI WILCOX WHEELER

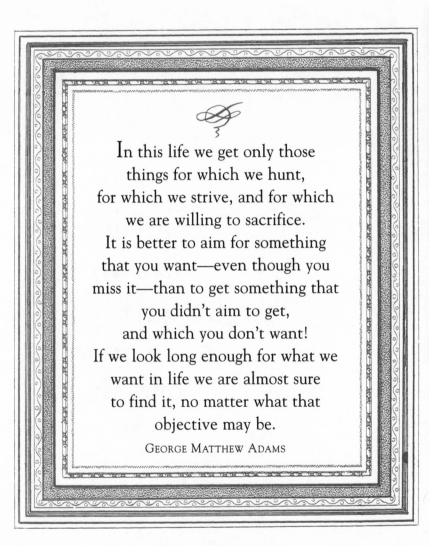

In this life we get only those
things for which we hunt,
for which we strive, and for which
we are willing to sacrifice.
It is better to aim for something
that you want—even though you
miss it—than to get something that
you didn't aim to get,
and which you don't want!
If we look long enough for what we
want in life we are almost sure
to find it, no matter what that
objective may be.

GEORGE MATTHEW ADAMS

I feel that the greatest reward for doing is the opportunity to do more.

JONAS SALK

Little Strokes, Fell great Oaks.

POOR RICHARD'S ALMANAC

But warm, eager, living life—to be rooted in life—to learn, to desire, to know, to feel, to think, to act. That is what I want. And nothing less. That is what I must try for.

KATHERINE MANSFIELD

Love the moment and the energy of that moment will spread beyond all boundaries.

CORITA KENT

Where there's a will there's a way.

PROVERB

I've had a few setbacks in my life, but I never gave up.

HARRY S. TRUMAN

Don't be afraid to take a big step if one is indicated.
You can't cross a chasm in two small jumps.

DAVID LLOYD GEORGE

You start at the beginning,
go on until you get to the end,
then stop.

LEWIS CARROLL

Never measure the height of a mountain,
until you have reached the top.
Then you will see how low it was.

DAG HAMMARSKJÖLD

He that climbs a ladder must begin at the first round.

SIR WALTER SCOTT

The older I get,
the more wisdom I find
in the ancient rule of taking
first things first—
a process which often
reduces the most complex
human problems to
manageable proportions.

DWIGHT D. EISENHOWER

The journey of a thousand

miles begins with one step.

LAO-TSE

That is the mark of a really admirable man:
steadfastness in the face of trouble.

LUDWIG VAN BEETHOVEN

Always dream and shoot higher than
you know you can do.

WILLIAM FAULKNER

Courage is very important.
Like a muscle, it is strengthened by use.

RUTH GORDON

Press on.
Nothing in the world can take the place of persistence.

RAY A. KROC

Life is like riding a bicycle.
You don't fall off unless you stop peddling.

CLAUDE PEPPER

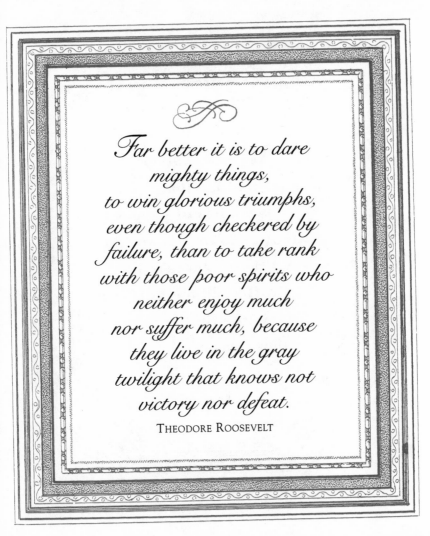

*Far better it is to dare
mighty things,
to win glorious triumphs,
even though checkered by
failure, than to take rank
with those poor spirits who
neither enjoy much
nor suffer much, because
they live in the gray
twilight that knows not
victory nor defeat.*

THEODORE ROOSEVELT

My grandfather
once told me that there
are two kinds of people:
those who do the work
and those who take the
credit. He told me to try to
be in the first group;
there was much less
competition there.

INDIRA GANDHI

Opportunity often goes unrecognized because it wears
overalls and often looks like work.

ANONYMOUS

The only place where success comes before work
is a dictionary.

VIDAL SASSOON

How do I work? I grope.

ALBERT EINSTEIN

I am a great believer in luck, and I find the harder I
work, the more I have of it.

STEPHEN LEACOCK

Everything comes to him who hustles while he waits.

THOMAS A. EDISON

Some people look at the
world and say "why?"

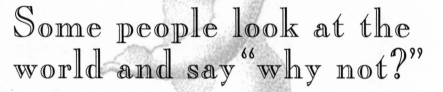

Some people look at the world and say "why not?"

GEORGE BERNARD SHAW

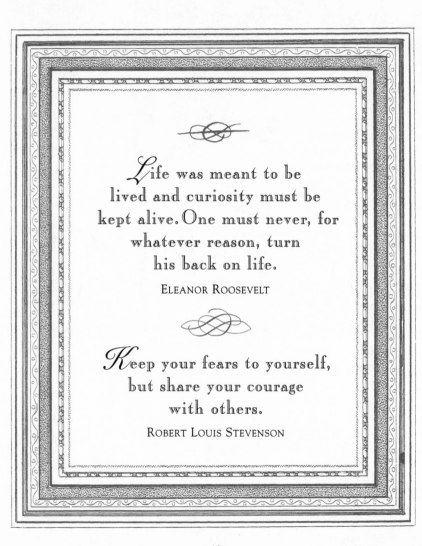

$\mathcal{L}$ife was meant to be
lived and curiosity must be
kept alive. One must never, for
whatever reason, turn
his back on life.

ELEANOR ROOSEVELT

$\mathcal{K}$eep your fears to yourself,
but share your courage
with others.

ROBERT LOUIS STEVENSON

Do what you know best; if you're a runner, run,
if you're a bell, ring.

IGNAS BERNSTEIN

Nothing will ever be attempted if all possible
objections must be first overcome.

SAMUEL JOHNSON

Think of yourself as on the threshold of unparalleled
success. A whole clear, glorious life lies before you.
Achieve! Achieve!

ANDREW CARNEGIE

There are many wonderful things that will never be
done if you do not do them.

HONORABLE CHARLES D. GILL

Mistakes are part of the dues one pays for a full life.

SOPHIA LOREN

What is worth doing is worth finishing. If it isn't worth finishing, why begin at all?

BALTASAR GRACIÁN

Life itself is the proper binge.

JULIA CHILD

First comes the sweat. Then comes the beauty—if you're very lucky and have said your prayers.

GEORGE BALANCHINE

Whenever you fall, pick up something.

OSWALD THEODORE AVERY

Keep your face to the sunshine and you cannot
see the shadow.

HELEN KELLER

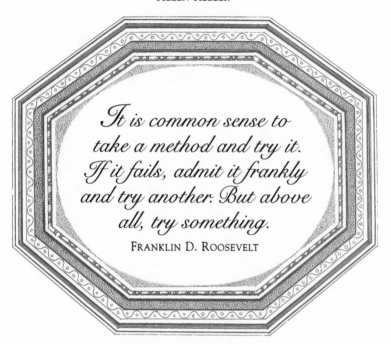

*It is common sense to
take a method and try it.
If it fails, admit it frankly
and try another. But above
all, try something.*

FRANKLIN D. ROOSEVELT

A person with a hundred interests is twice as alive as
one with only fifty and four times as alive as the man
who has only twenty-five.

NORMAN VINCENT PEALE

$\mathcal{H}$old fast to dreams,

a broken-winged bird

for if dreams die, life is

that cannot fly. LANGSTON HUGHES

No one knows what it is that he can do until he tries.

PUBLILIUS SYRUS

Do all the good you can,
in all the ways you can,
to all the souls you can,
in every place you can,
at all the times you can,
with all the zeal you can,
as long as ever you can.

JOHN WESLEY

When love and skill work together,
expect a masterpiece.

JOHN RUSKIN

An optimist is a person who sees a green light
everywhere, while the pessimist sees only the red
stoplight. . . .The truly wise person is colorblind.

ALBERT SCHWEITZER

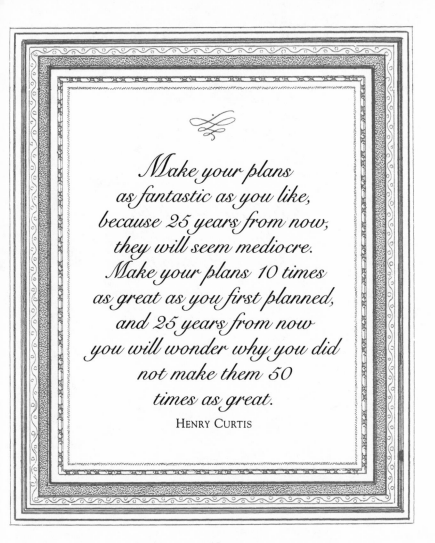

*Make your plans
as fantastic as you like,
because 25 years from now,
they will seem mediocre.
Make your plans 10 times
as great as you first planned,
and 25 years from now
you will wonder why you did
not make them 50
times as great.*

HENRY CURTIS

The only joy in the world is to begin.

CESARE PAVESE

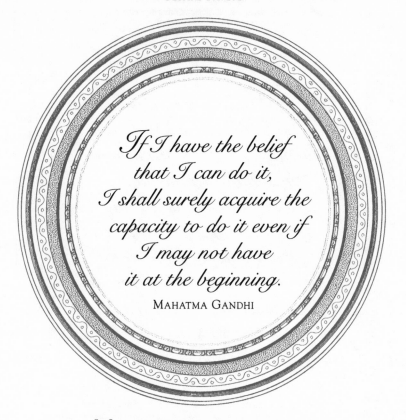

*If I have the belief
that I can do it,
I shall surely acquire the
capacity to do it even if
I may not have
it at the beginning.*

MAHATMA GANDHI

Make hay while the sun shines.

PROVERB

The greatest discovery of my generation is that a human being can change his life by changing his attitude of mind.

WILLIAM JAMES

If at first you don't succeed,
Try, try again.

WILLIAM EDWARD HICKSON

A rock pile ceases to be a rock pile the moment a single man contemplates it, bearing within him the image of a cathedral.

ANTOINE DE SAINT-EXUPÉRY

Whenever you are asked if you can do a job, tell 'em, "Certainly I can!"—and get busy and find out how to do it.

THEODORE ROOSEVELT

Miracles happen to those

who believe in them.

BERNARD BERENSON

If there's a book you really want to read but it hasn't been written yet, then you must write it.

TONI MORRISON

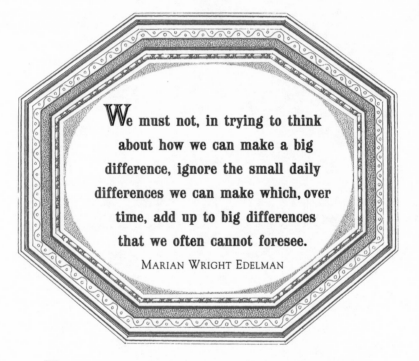

We must not, in trying to think about how we can make a big difference, ignore the small daily differences we can make which, over time, add up to big differences that we often cannot foresee.

MARIAN WRIGHT EDELMAN

Those who bring sunshine to the lives of others cannot keep it from themselves.

JAMES M. BARRIE

Never doubt that a small group of thoughtful
committed citizens can change the world.
Indeed it's the only thing that ever has.

MARGARET MEAD

If you find it in your heart to care for somebody else,
you will have succeeded.

MAYA ANGELOU

The World is a great mirror. It reflects back to you
what you are. If you are loving, if you are friendly, if
you are helpful, the World will prove loving and
friendly and helpful to you. The World is what you are.

THOMAS DREIER

It is one of the most beautiful compensations of life
that no man can sincerely try to help another,
without helping himself.

JOHN P. WEBSTER

Promise yourself to be so strong that nothing can disturb your peace of mind.
To speak of health, happiness, and prosperity to every person that you meet. To make all your friends aware of the special qualities within them.
To look at the sunny side of every thing and let your optimism work to make your dreams come true.
To think, work for, and expect only the best.
To be just as enthusiastic about the success of others, as you are about your own. To forget past mistakes and press on towards a greater future. To wear a cheerful countenance at all times, as a smile radiates warmth and love. To give so much time to the improvement of yourself that you have no time left to criticize others. To be too wise for worry, too tolerant for anger, and too courageous for fear.
To Be Happy.

Anonymous

I am only one, but still I am one; I
cannot do everything, but still I can
do something; and because I cannot
do everything I will not refuse to do
the something that I can do.

EDWARD E. HALE

To be nobody-but-yourself—
in a world which is doing its best,
night and day, to make you
everybody but yourself—
means to fight the hardest battle
which any human being can fight,
and never stop fighting.

E. E. CUMMINGS

'Tis always morning somewhere in the world.

RICHARD HENRY HORNE

 Hope is the thing with feathers
That perches in the soul
And sings the tune without the words
And never stops, at all.

EMILY DICKINSON

Take time to be friendly—
    It is the road to happiness.
Take time to dream—
    It is hitching your wagon to a star.
Take time to love and to be loved—
    It is the privilege of the gods.
Take time to look around—
    It is too short a day to be selfish.
Take time to laugh—
    It is the music of the soul.

OLD ENGLISH PRAYER